Seaford Timeline

Events in Seaford Through the Reigns of the M
From 1066 to 2002

Seaford Coat of Arms showing, *dexter,* the two half lions/half ships from the arms of Hastings, sinister, the eagle from the Aquila arms and base, the ship from the arms of the Cinque Ports. The motto, *E Ventis Vires* means 'Strength from the Winds'

Researched and compiled by members of
SEAFORD MUSEUM and HERITAGE SOCIETY

First published in 2002

© Copyright 2002 Seaford Museum and Heritage Society

ISBN: 1 902170 10 5

No part of this publication may be reproduced, stored in a retrieval system, transmitted in any form or by any means electronic, mechanical, photocopying, recording or otherwise without the prior permission of the Seaford Museum and Heritage Society.

Compiled and edited by Mick Barrett
Published by the Seaford Museum and Heritage Society,
in aid of funds for Seaford Museum

SEAFORD MUSEUM and HERITAGE SOCIETY
Postal address: c/o Tourist Information Centre, 25 Clinton Place, Seaford, East Sussex BN25 1NP

Tel: 01323-898222 E-mail: museumseaford@tinyonline.co.uk Web-site: www.seafordmuseum.org

Printed by Tansleys Printers
19 Broad Street, Seaford, East Sussex BN25 1LS
Tel: 01323 891019 Fax: 01323 899484

Contents

Acknowledgments		4
Introduction		5
William I	1066 - 1087	7
William II	1087 - 1100	7
Henry I	1100 - 1135	9
Stephen	1135 - 1154	9
Henry II	1154 - 1189	11
Richard I	1189 - 1199	11
John	1199 - 1216	13
Henry III	1216 - 1272	13
Edward I	1272 - 1307	15
Edward II	1307 - 1327	15
Edward III	1327 - 1377	17
Richard II	1377 - 1399	17
Henry IV	1399 - 1413	19
Henry V	1413 - 1422	19
Henry VI	1422 - 1461	21
Edward IV	1461 - 1483	21
Edward V	April-August 1483	23
Richard III	1483 - 1485	23
Henry VII	1485 - 1509	25
Henry VIII	1509 - 1547	25
Edward VI	1547 - 1553	27
Mary	1553 - 1558	27
Elizabeth I	1558 - 1603	29
James I	1603 - 1625	31
Charles I	1625 - 1649	31
Cromwell	1649 - 1660	33
Charles II	1660 - 1685	33
James II	1685 - 1688	35
William III & Mary II	1688 - 1702	35
Anne	1702 - 1714	37
George I	1714 - 1727	39
George II	1727 - 1760	39
George III	1760 - 1811	41
The Regency	1811 - 1820	47
George IV	1820 - 1830	47
William IV	1830 - 1837	47
Victoria	1837 - 1901	49
Edward VII	1901 - 1910	53
George V	1910 - 1936	53
Edward VIII	1936 - 1936	55
George VI	1936 - 1952	55
Elizabeth II	1952 -	57
Seaford Museum		62

Acknowledgments

Details of most of the events listed here were originally in a Seaford Museum publication entitled "Seaford Chronological History" first produced by Joan Astell, which has been upgraded several times by John Odam. Further details may be found in other publications, notably in the "Seaford History Book" by John Odam, which may be obtained through the Seaford Museum of Local History. The Introduction to this book is taken from his "Bygone Seaford".

Most of the illustrations (up to George V) are from a 1935 collection of Player's Cigarette cards. The others were obtained from public domain information on the Internet. Most of the line drawings are by David Taylor of Seaford Museum.

Thanks are due to many members of the Museum for providing inputs and advice and to Steve Benz of SB Publications for his guidance.

New historical information continues to come to light and readers are encouraged to include their own notes on the following pages. The Museum would also welcome further information which can be included in future issues.

Introduction

The history of any place is affected, often dictated, by its geographical location, and there is no better example of this than the town of Seaford. Men settled in Seaford because it was on the coast and on a river estuary and it is this which has shaped its history at every period since. Flint implements have been found in and around the town, indicating Stone Age occupation of the area, and part of a large Iron Age hill fort is still discernible on Seaford Head in spite of considerable cliff erosion. There was a substantial Roman villa at Eastbourne and a Roman burial ground on the present Seaford Head golf course. Roman funerary vessels and Roman coins have been found locally so it would seem that Seaford was inhabited periodically, if not constantly, by Ancient Britons right through to the Romano-British period.

The first written evidence of Seaford comes from the Saxon occupation in the fifth century when *Sefordt* was mentioned in early chronicles inferring a ford near the sea or perhaps a fiord of the sea. An eighth-century transaction mentions a town as being *Super Juvium Saforda* or 'on the river Saforda', presumably the river Ouse which then flowed into the sea at Seaford. Although the town's earliest history must remain vague, the sea and the river Ouse are very real and we do know how nature used these two geographical features to set Seaford literally on the map. In fact, to understand Seaford's eminence in the Middle Ages and its political significance in the 18th century we simply have to look at the winds and tides in Seaford Bay.

Although Seaford is on the south coast, it actually faces south-west so is at the mercy of the gales coming in directly from the Atlantic. Many centuries ago the tides and prevailing winds gradually built up a great shingle bank right across Seaford Bay from the cliffs at Meeching (Newhaven) to the cliffs at Seaford Head. As this barrier grew, the river Ouse was diverted eastwards until it drove its way out into the sea at Splash Point under Seaford Head and the very low-lying area behind the bank was flooded and formed a natural harbour. It is difficult to picture this in the Seaford of today until one remembers that in Saxon times the cliff ends at Meeching and Seaford projected much further out into the sea, so that the shingle barrier was considerably further seaward than the present shoreline. A look at a conjectural map of the bay in that period superimposed over Seaford of the 1980s shows how the old river Ouse flowed inland, rounding the spurs and lapping into the ancient Ice Age valleys of Bishopstone, Hawth and Blatchington.

Certainly this happened long before the Norman Conquest and we know that by the early 13th century Seaford was a Cinque Port and senior limb of the head port of Hastings, the other head ports at that time being Sandwich, Dover, Romney and Hythe. During its most prosperous period the port of Seaford gave employment in fishing, ship building, provisioning of ships and a two-way trade with the continent, importing wines and exporting wool from the large flocks of Downland sheep. This book provides a quick reference to the English monarchs from William the Conqueror up to our present Queen. Important (and trivial) events for the town of Seaford are entered in chronological order within the reigns of these kings and queens of England showing the growth and decline of the town. To assist with historical context during these years, important national or global events are also included.

National and Other Events

During the reign of William I, also known as William the Conqueror, (m. Matilda of Flanders)

1066   Battle of Hastings leading to the Norman Conquest.

1081   Tower of London started.

1085   Doomsday (Domesday) Book.

Building Castles

During the reign of William II, also known as William Rufus

1096   First crusade founded Christian kingdom in Jerusalem.

Seaford Events

William I
1066 – 1087

1086　Bishopstone shown in Doomsday Book as the property of the Bishop of Chichester. Seaford shares the distinction of **NOT** being mentioned along with London, Liverpool and Bristol!

William II
1087 - 1100

1090　Building of the Parish Church (St. Leonard's) is started.

National and Other Events

During the reign of Henry I (m. Matilda of Scotland)

1106   Battle of Tenchebrai and Conquest of Normandy.

1116   War with France (to 1119).

1119   Order of the Knights Templars founded.

1123   St. Bartholomew's Hospital founded.

1135   Rebellion in Wales.

During the reign of Stephen (m. Maude of Boulogne)

1138   Battle of the Standard.

1141   Battle of Lincoln.

1147   Second Crusade (St. Bernard).

1153   Treaty of Wallingford and end of Civil War.

Seaford Events

Henry I
1100 - 1135

1120   North and South aisles are added to the Church.

Stephen
1135 – 1154

1138   By Charter, the Third Earl de Warenne grants rights in Seaford to the monks of Lewes Priory.

1147   The Hospital of St. Leonard is founded by Roger de Fraxineto.

National and Other Events

During the reign of Henry II, also known as Henry Plantaganet (m. Eleanor of Aquitaine)

1158   Building of Dover Castle.

1162   Becket made Archbishop.

1170   Murder of Becket.

1174   Great Rebellion. Start building Wells Cathedral.

During the reign of Richard I, Coeur de Lion (m. Berengaria of Navarre)

1190   Third Crusade.

1191   Robin Hood.

1192   Richard in captivity. War with France.

Seaford Events

Henry II
1154 - 1189

1172 A further grant of 7 acres is given by Roger de Fraxineto.
1182 Seaford Church granted to the Dean and Chapter of Chichester.

Richard I
1189 - 1199

1190 Revenue from a windmill in Bishopstone is given to a college in Chichester. Believed to be the first reference to a windmill in England.

National and Other Events

During the reign of John (m. Isabella of Angouleme)

1203   Death of Arthur.

1204   Loss of Normandy.

1212   John excommunicated.

During the reign of Henry III (m. Eleanor of Provence)

1225   Magna Carta.

1245   Westminster Abbey built 1245 - 1269.

1257   Simon de Montfort, National Rising.

1264   Battle of Lewes.

1265   Battle of Evesham and Simon's Parliament.

Seaford Events

John
1199 - 1216

1199 King John is believed to have landed at Seaford.
1200 The Parish Church is heightened by the addition of the clerestory.
1216 King John and his retinue stay overnight in Seaford and the King writes a letter praising the loyalty of the Men of Seaford.

Henry III
1216 - 1272

1224 An order to prepare for service at sea is addressed independently to Seaford.
1229 The first mention of Seaford as a limb of the Cinque Port of Hastings.
1260 The Hospital of St. James at Sutton-by-Seaford is founded.
1263 Complaint by the Burghers of Seaford that the three Bailiffs of the Earl de Warenne have increased the port tolls payable to the Earl. They take the matter to Court at Shoreham and have the original rates restored.
1264 Henry III passes through Seaford.

During this period, a Baronial Seal for Seaford was introduced. (The Aquila Seal)

National and Other Events

During the reign of Edward I (m. Eleanor of Castile)

1274   Conquest of Wales (1274 – 1282).

1275   First Statute of Westminster.

1294   William Wallace. Attempted conquest of Scotland and Scotland's alliance with France (lasts to 1494).

1300   Start of Border Wars with Scotland (last to 1550).

1306   Robert the Bruce crowned in Scotland.

During the reign of Edward II (m. Isabella of France)

1314   Battle of Bannockburn.

1315   Famine.

1322   Battle of Boroughbridge. Execution of Thomas of Lancaster.

1325   Queen obtains French help.

Seaford Events

Edward I
1272 - 1307

- **1272** All Jews in Seaford and Lewes taxed two shillings (10p).
- **1287** William Potel hangs himself in the Hermitage at Seaford.
- **1288** Sea coal is obtained from Seaford for use in lime burning at Willingdon.
- **1291** The levy on Seaford Prebend is £4.13s.4d. (£4.67.) and on Sutton is £26.13s.4d. (£26.67.).
- **1295** Systems of coast guards are now introduced as Scotland is in alliance with France.
- **1298** Seaford is granted the right to elect two members to Parliament. Geofree Cuckoo and William Hobey are the first members.
- **1298** Seaford is ordered to send a ship to both Berwick and Dublin but ignores the order.
- **1301** The King orders a fair to be held in Seaford on the 25th July each year.

Edward II
1307 - 1327

- **1309** Seaford is ordered to supply one ship in support of the war against Scotland.
- **1323** Seaford is ordered to supply one ship to carry troops to Aquitaine.
- **1324** Edward II stays at Bishopstone.
- **1325** Seaford's complement of ships over 50 tons is assessed as one ship and 37 men.

National and Other Events

During the reign of Edward III (m. Philippa of Hainault)

1330   Flemings settle in Norwich and add to importance of wool trade.

1333   Battle of Halidon Hill.

1338   Start of the Hundred Years War with France (lasts to 1453).

1347   Capture of Calais.

1348   Black Death (1348-9).   (Contemporary illustration)

1373   English translation of the Bible.

1376   Death of the Black Prince.

During the reign of Richard II son of the Black Prince (m. 1. Anne of Bohemia, 2. Isabella of France)

1381   Peasants' Revolt led by Wat Tyler.

1384   Death of John Wyclif, leader of the Lollards.

Edward III
1327 – 1377

Seaford Events

1341 Seaford is described as being "damaged often and in many ways by the assaults of the French and some of its inhabitants wounded and slain."

1342 Seaford attends the advisory Council of the Cinque Ports to combat the problem of piracy.

1348 Seaford sends three ships to the French (100 years) war. The Black Death (plague) affects the whole country.

1349 Four fifths of the parish of Exceat are dead, and it is deserted.

1350 Battle of Poitiers takes place at which Sir John Pelham accepts the French King's sword in surrender and adopts *The Buckle* in his coat of arms.

1352 A Spanish ship seized in the port of Seaford is taken into the King's use.

1357 Seaford is described as "for the most part burnt down and devastated by pestilence and calamities of war so that the townsmen have become so few and so poor that they can neither bear their burdens or undertake the defence of the town against its enemies."

1368 The Hospital of St. Leonard is destroyed by inundation by the sea.

1368 French raiders burn Sutton vicarage.

Richard II
1377 - 1399

1380 The King is petitioned by "his poor lieges of Seaford" for postponement or remission of taxes "as their houses and goods have been burnt and destroyed by the sudden raids of the French enemies, in which town there were as many as 200 burgesses dwelling before the said destruction".

National and Other Events

During the reign of Henry IV (m. 1. Mary Bohun, 2. Joanna of Navarre)

1399 Richard deposed by Henry IV, first of the Lancastrian kings of England. Westminster Hall completed.

1400 Owen Glendower revolts in Wales. Death of Chaucer.

1402 Birth of Joan of Arc (1402 – 1431).

During the reign of Henry V (m. Catherine of France)

1415 Use of guns and gunpowder in Europe (China used explosives in warfare in 1161).

1415 Battle of Agincourt.

Seaford Events

Henry IV
1399 - 1413

1400 Seaford's parliamentary representation lapses for 241 years.

Henry V
1413 - 1422

1421 Robert, Lord Poynings and Sir John Pelham are appointed commissioners for repairing the banks of the coast between Meeching (Newhaven) and Seaford.

National and Other Events

During the reign of Henry VI (m. Margaret of Anjou)

1431   Burning of Joan of Arc.

1450   Jack Cade's Rebellion.

1452   Birth of Leonardo da Vinci.

1453   Battle of Castillon with the defeat of the English and end of the Hundred Years War.

During the reign of Edward IV (m. Elizabeth Woodville)

1455   First battle of St. Albans and start of the War of the Roses.

1470   Warwick "The Kingmaker" turns Lancastrian and dethrones Edward IV.

1471   Battle of Barnet. Edward IV kills Warwick (see right).

1473   Birth of Michelangelo.

1476   Caxton's printing press (Gutenburg had already been printing in Germany since 1440 and the Chinese centuries earlier).

Seaford Events

Henry VI
1422 - 1461

- **1422** A licence is obtained to Wall and Ditch the town (but not carried out).
- **1439** Seaford appears in a schedule of benefices accustomed to pay tithes but which have been impoverished by inundations, floods and conflagrations.
- **1450** Robert Poynings of Sutton, Richard Carpenter, Bailiff of Seaford, seven yeomen, a barber, a husbandman and a butcher from the town join Jack Cade's rebellion and are personally named in the later pardons given on condition that they return peaceably to their homes.

Edward IV
1461 - 1483

- **1461** The King gives the Manor of Seaford to his Queen, Elizabeth Woodville.

National and Other Events

During the reign of Edward V

1483   Edward was only 12 years old when his father died.

1483   Finish of painting in the Sistine Chapel by Botticelli, Ghirlandaio and Perugino.

1483   Murder of the Princes in the Tower (Edward V and his brother).

The mark of William Caxton in books of this period.

During the reign of Richard III (m. Anne Neville)

1483   Richard Duke of Gloucester seizes the throne.

1483   Organisation of the Spanish Inquisition.

1485   Battle of Bosworth Field. Richard dies on the battlefield fighting against Henry.

**Edward V
April-August
1483**

**Richard III
1483 - 1485**

Seaford Events

Depiction of a printers workshop in this period (Not in Seaford).

National and Other Events

During the reign of Henry VII, Tudor (m. Elizabeth of York)

1485   Henry assumes the crown after defeating Richard. Start of the Tudor period.

1486   Discovery of the Cape of Good Hope.

1487   Lambert Sinnel's rebellion.

1491   War with France.

1492   Columbus discovers America.

1497   Following encouragement from Henry VII, John Cabot lands in North America.

During the reign of Henry VIII, (m. 1. Katherine of Arragon, 2. Anne Boleyn, 3. Jane Seymour, 4. Anne of Cleves, 5. Katherine Howard, 6. Katherine Parr)

1520   Field of the Cloth of Gold.

1521   Martin Luther outlawed by the Diet of Worms.

1528   Death of Albrecht Duerer.

1534   Henry VIII asserts control of the English church.

1536   Dissolution of smaller monasteries followed by larger monasteries in 1539.

1546   Death of Martin Luther.

Seaford Events

Henry VII
1485 – 1509

1508 Sutton church is annexed to Seaford.

Seal of the Cinque Port of Seaford

Henry VIII
1509 - 1547

1539 Commissioners surveying the coast report that Seaford is no longer worthy of important defence, although the harbour still accommodates smaller ships.
1540 First mention of St. Leonard as patron saint of Seaford parish church.
1544 Seaford is granted a charter by the King, confirming the ancient rights and duties it enjoyed as a cinque port.
1545 The last French raid on this part of the coast is repelled by local people led by Sir Nicholas Pelham whose family coat of arms gives the name *The Buckle* to that part of the beach.

National and Other Events

During the reign of Edward VI

1547 Edward was only 9 years old and Hertford, then renamed Duke of Somerset was nominated as Protector. This was the start of several years of Protestant / Catholic conflicts.

1553 Edward dies of consumption.
Northumberland fears Mary (the legal successor) and proclaimed Lady Jane Grey as queen. However a general revolt supports Mary Tudor as the daughter of Henry VIII.

During the reign of Mary I (m. Phillip of Spain)

1554 Wyatt's rebellion. Executions of Northumberland and Lady Jane Grey.
Princess Elizabeth (the next queen) imprisoned in the Tower for a short time.

1555 Lattimer and Ridley burned at the stake (Like many during this reign charged as heretics).

1558 Mary (Stuart) Queen of Scots marries the Dauphin. Mary I dies aged 42.

1558 Calais lost to the French.

Edward VI
1547 - 1553

Seaford Events

1548   A Royal Commission mentions Seaford as being seriously affected by a shortage of timber to build groynes.

Mary
1553 - 1558

National and Other Events

During the reign of Elizabeth I

1558 Elizabeth succeeds her sister.

1561 Mary Stuart Queen of Scots returns to Scotland.

1564 Birth of William Shakespeare and death of Michelangelo.

1565 Mary Stuart marries Darnley.

1567 Murder of Darnley. Mary marries Bothwell.

1568 Mary escapes to England and imprisoned.

1570 Pope excommunicates Elizabeth.

1577 Drake sets out to sail around the world. Returns 1580.

1582 Introduction of the Gregorian calendar by Pope Gregory XIII.

1587 Execution of Mary Queen of Scots.

1588 Defeat of the Spanish armada.

Seaford Events

Elizabeth I
1558 - 1603

1559	Seaford Parish Register begins.
1562	Seaford Town Hall is built. (Still existing in South Street) Seaford Corporation minutes are available from this date in County Record Office.
1565	The population of the Town is down to 38 householders, including seven fishermen, and the town has only one boat.
1578	The "Pillory Tree" stands at the corner of Broad Street and North Street. An inn known as the "Old Tree" is subsequently built on the site (demolished in 1965).
1579	Legend says this is the date of a great storm, which caused the outflow of the Ouse to be diverted from Splash Point to Meeching thus creating a New Haven. In fact the New Haven was constructed to relieve the regular flooding higher up the Ouse valley.
1580	Sir John Pelham inherits the Manor of Bishopstone.
1592	The last known reference to the existence of a shipwright in the town of Seaford.
1592	By Royal Charter, Elizabeth grants 30 acres of land, known as the Beamelands or Salts to the people of Seaford in perpetuity. (Only a part remains behind the Martello Tower).
1594	The Ducking stool, the Pillory and the Butts (for archery practice) are reported to be in a state of disrepair.
1596	Seaford is reported as having "neither haven, creke or other landing place but the stone beche only and hath householders 38, fishermen 7". There is also reported one boat of 1 tons named Nell and one piece of ordnance.
1600	All able-bodied men with a knowledge of the sea are exempted from impressment as soldiers.
1601	Brickworks are in existence at Lion's Place, Blatchington Road and between Hawth Hill and Kimberly Road.

National and Other Events

During the reign of James I (m. Anne of Denmark)

1605   Gunpowder Plot.

1607   Colonisation of Virginia by London company. Jamestown founded.

1613   Michael Romonov becomes Tsar of Russia. The first of the Romonov dynasty.

1616   Death of Shakespeare.

1620   The Pilgrim Fathers settle in New England.

During the reign of Charles I (m. Henrietta Maria of France)

1628   Petition of Right by Commons to Charles. Then Dissolution of third Parliament. Charles begins "Personal Rule".

1639   First Bishops' War. The King settles terms with the Scots.

1640   Second Bishops' War. The King defeated by the Scots. Long Parliament begins and abolition of royal prerogatives.

1641   Massacre of Protestants in Ireland. Remonstrance of Commons to the King.

1642   Charles attempts to arrest the "Five Members" Start of Civil War.

1646   Charles surrenders to the Scots and handed over to Parliament the next year.

1648   Second Civil War. New Model Army defeats Scots and Royalists.

1649   The King is beheaded in Whitehall.

Seaford Events

James I
1603 - 1625

1603   Place House is built by the Gratwick family on the north side of the junction of Place Lane and Broad Street.

1605   A fine of 3s.4d (approx. 18p) is to be paid by anyone "flinging carion or filth into the old haven or anywhere about the town".

1619   Seaford's muster roll shows the Trained Band to be equipped thus: "27 muskets, 5 Corsletts and 13 Bill and Sculls, and every musket hath 2lbs of powder, 2lbs of shot and match as was commanded".

1623   An inquest is held on Thomas Castreat, accidentally shot in "Chingtinge Lanes" by Arthur Pollarde, Gentleman.

1624   Mr Elfick accused of taking and distributing wines from a wreck.

Charles I
1625 - 1649

1633   John Baker and John Chambers examined regarding stealing from wrecks.

1641   The Town reclaims its old parliamentary representation (2 seats).

1642   Two Seaford men are fined "or to be whipped" for selling ale without a licence. John Beane gives a sacramental flagon to St.Leonard's Church. (Flagon now in the British Museum).

1643   Goody Rance is ducked as a scold and Elizabeth Kenchley is whipped for a "pickory" (a theft to the value of 7d).

National and Other Events

During the Commonwealth, Oliver Cromwell & Richard Cromwell

- **1651** Charles II invades England.
- **1652** Start of first Anglo-Dutch war. Ends 1654.
- **1653** Cromwell becomes Protector.
- **1658** Cromwell dies naming his eldest son, Richard, to succeed him as Protector.
- **1659** Samuel Pepys begins to keep a diary. Dissolution of Richard's Parliament.
- **1660** Fall of the Protectorate, mainly by the army, which opened the way for Restoration of the Monarchy.

During the reign of Charles II (m. Catherine of Braganza)

- **1660** Formation of The Royal Society.
- **1665** The great plague.
- **1666** The great fire of London. Newton discovery of the law of gravitation.
- **1673** The Test Act deprives English Catholics and Non-conformists of public office. Death of Molliere.
- **1678** "Popish Plot" by Titus Oates virtually ousted the king for two years.
- **1681** Oxford Parliament. King begins to rule without Parliament.
- **1683** The Rye House Plot to assassinate the king was betrayed and many of Charles' opponents were executed.
- **1685** Despite all the plots against him, the King died naturally of a apoplexy.

Seaford Events

The Commonwealth. (Cromwell) 1649 - 1659

- **1650** The Old House (High Street) and Rose Cottage (South Street) are built.
- **1650** No more Freemen of the Town are to be appointed ' until our number of freemen be lessened to ye number of eighteene'.
- **1655** Fishing rights in the 'old haven' are let to John Swane for 20s per annum.
- **1657** Thomas Harrison is elected bailiff of the town. The family held the office 48 times in the next 190 years.

Charles II 1660 - 1685

- **1661** Sir William Thomas and Sir Thomas Dyke elected to parliament.

National and Other Events

During the reign of James II (m. 1. Anne Hyde, 2. Mary of Modena)

1685   The Monmouth rebellion, Monmouth, son of Charles II, defeated by James II and executed.

1688   Following years of the King's suppression of Protestants, William of Orange is invited to take the throne with his wife Mary, who was a granddaughter of Charles II. He accepts and deposes James who flees to Ireland.

During the reign of William III and Mary II

1692   Massacre of Glencoe.

1694   Bank of England founded.

1695   Freedom of the press in England.

Contemporary poster welcoming the new king

Seaford Events

James II
1685 - 1688

William III
& Mary II
1688 – 1702

1690 Anglo-Dutch fleet beaten by the French off Beachy Head.

National and Other Events

During the reign of Queen Anne (m. Prince George of Denmark)

1704   Gibraltar taken by Rooke.

1707   Act of Union. English and Scottish Parliaments united.

1710   Tory government in England.

Anne
1702 - 1714

1703   A disastrous storm hits Seaford and the sea is reported to reach the basement of 'The Plough' in Church Street.

1710   The muster roll details 3 Officers, 2 Sergeants and 33 men ready and nominated to bear arms in the defence of Seaford.

1712   Thomas Tufton of 'The Old House' dies while serving as Bailiff and his place is taken by *Smyter Styver* for the rest of the year.

1712   The last documentary mention of Seaford's market.

1713   Seaford's window tax is documented for 1713/14. One of only two such records known for Sussex. (The other being Petworth 1732).

National and Other Events

During the reign of George I (Hanoverian) (m. Sophia Dorothea of Zell)

1715   Jacobite rising defeated.

1720   South Sea Bubble.

1723   Death of Christopher Wren.

During the reign of George II (m. Caroline of Brandenburg-Anspach)

1729   Methodists begin at Oxford.

1733   Invention of the flying shuttle by John Kay.

1738   Lorraine ceded to France.

1743   Battle of Dettingen. Last time a king commands his army in the field. Defeats French.

Seaford Events

George I
1714 - 1727

- **1714** Thomas Pelham-Holles comes of age and takes his seat in the House of Lords. As Duke of Newcastle he continues to dominate the life and politics of Seaford until his death in 1768.
Talland House (now the site of Talland Parade) is built.
The keeping of geese on the common is forbidden.
- **1717** Henry Pelham (Newcastle's younger brother) is elected MP for Seaford. He later becomes Leader of the House of Commons.
- **1722** Sir Phillip Yorke is elected MP for Seaford. He later becomes Lord Hardwicke and is the Attorney General.
- **1724** Seaford's population is now only 20 families.
- **1726** A 'Humble Address' is sent to George I congratulating him on his defeat of the Jacobite uprising.

George II
1727 - 1760

- **1727** Another 'Humble Address' is sent from Seaford, to George II congratulating him on his accession to the throne.
- **1728** The cost of the fishing rights in the 'Old Haven' is increased to 22s. (£1.10p).
- **1733** A by-election is held at which William Hay (a cousin by marriage to the Duke of Newcastle) is elected MP for Seaford.
- **1733** Saxon Lodge is built in Saxon Lane for a member of the Beane family.
- **1735** The local Poor Rate is now 6d.
- **1739** Barbara Joplin, Seaford's oldest inhabitant, (born in 1632 before the start of the Civil War) dies aged 107.
- **1740** The fishermen of Seaford are exempted from the 'Press Gang' for this season.
- **1744** Another 'Humble Address' is sent to the King encouraging his resistance to the Jacobite rebellion.

National and Other Events

During the reign of George II (m. Caroline of Brandenburg-Anspach) (cont.)

1745   Jacobite rebellion under Prince Charles Edward – Initial success over Prestonpans. March to Derby.

1746   Battle of Cullodon. Jacobites destroyed by Cumberland.

1750   Death of Johan Sebastian Bach.

1752   Britain adopts New Style (Gregorian) Calendar.

1759   Capture of Quebec.

During the reign of George III (m. Charlotte of Mecklenburg-Streilitz)

1763   Peace of Paris gives British colonial gains making the British Empire at its greatest.

1764   John Wilkes expelled from Commons. Invention of the Spinning Jenny by James Hargreaves.

Seaford Events

George II
1727 - 1760
(cont.)

1744	£1. 16s. 10d spent on repairing Seaford's one remaining gun.
1747	A bitter contest in the general election between the Pelham candidates and the Gages of Firle Place leads to a debate in the House of Commons on corruption in the election at Seaford. The Pelham candidates, William Pitt and William Hay win.
1747	The 'Nympha Americana', a Spanish prize, is wrecked at Crowlink.
1750	George II says of Newcastle and his protégés Henry Pelham and Lord Hardwicke, 'They are the only Ministers, the rest are for show'.
1758	It is reported that rain has fallen every day for 29 days!

George III
1760 - 1811

1761	The building of Blatchington Battery starts and the Tide Mills Bill receives Parliamentary approval.
1762	Mr French is fined 18d for using false weights. Mr Templeman is paid 1s.4d for beating a drum in celebration of war with Spain and Robert Stone (bailiff) pays only 14d rent for a house on the Common and the old Gun Barn.
1763	Rex v Stone. A case in the King's bench alleges that Robert Stone holds the office of Bailiff illegally. (The Bailiff wins.)
1763	A 13year old boy is killed by Mr Farncomb's jack-ass wheel at Blatchington. His head caught between the pump wheel and a post.
Sand and shingle taken from the beach to be charged at 6d per load but John Osbourne to have it free (for 20s a year).
1764	Rex v Washer. A similar case to that against R Stone the previous year. The Bailiff wins again.
Thomas Swaine of The Old Tree Inn-keeper family dies leaving a 'handsome fortune' from his services as major Domo (and political informant) to his master, The Duke of Newcastle at Bishopstone Place.

During the reign of George III (m. Charlotte of Mecklenburg-Streilitz) (cont.)

1768   founding of The Royal Academy of Arts.

1769   Richard Arkwright erects a spinning mill.

1770   James Cook discovers New South Wales in Australia.

1773   Boston Tea Party.

1776   American Declaration of Independence.

1783   William Pitt the Younger becomes Prime Minister (lived for a time in Seaford).
First flights in a hot-air balloon by the Montgolfier brothers in France and Hydrogen balloon by Charles in England.

1787   Drafting of the American Constitution.

1789   Start of the French Revolution. Storming of the Bastille.
George Washington the first President of the United States.

Seaford Events

George III
1760 - 1811
(cont.)

1767	Stone's house in the Crouch is built.
1768	The death of the Duke of Newcastle sees the virtual cessation of political sinecures for his local supporters in Seaford.
1769	Harison's customs cutter seizes a smuggled cargo of rum, gin and tea etc. The haul is auctioned. Sutton Mill (Eastbourne Road) is built.
1771	Salary of the Town Clerk is £3.5s.0d. per annum. Guestling of the Cinque Ports is attended by the Bailiff, two Jurats, one Freeman and the Town Clerk. (Normally not more than two people attend for Seaford.) A child, John Earl, meets an untimely death in a copper of hot water. During a fracas at the Town Hall Robert Jones, a shoemaker, takes away the town chest containing the Charter. An attempt to read the Riot Act is unsuccessful.
1777	Francis Grose, diarist, visits Seaford. (Diary in British Museum.)
1778	During work on the church 2 coffin stones & 1 coffin containing 16 skulls is found.
1779	Escaping from a French prison three Englishmen, having stolen a small boat, land at Seaford where they sell the boat for £1.17s.0d. £1.19s.6d. is spent on a new pair of stocks.
1783	Corsica Hall at Wellingham is purchased by Thomas Harben and moved by barge to Seaford where it is rebuilt on the hillock overlooking the old harbour. It is renamed 'Millberg House' (but is once again known as Corsica Hall today).
1784	A turbot weighing 15lbs is caught at Seaford and presented to Mr Harben. The church clock is moved to the south side of the tower.
1789	A riot at the town hall, organised by T.H.B.Oldfield – a political reformer/agitator.

Seaford in 1785
By Samual Heronymous Grimm

National and Other Events

During the reign of George III (m. Charlotte of Mecklenburg-Streilitz) (cont.)

1792 Denmark becomes the first country to ban slave trading.
France becomes a Republic.

1796 First Italian campaign of Napoleon Bonaparte.

1798 Napoleon Bonaparte battle of the Nile.

1800 Parliamentary Union of Great Britain and Ireland.

1804 Napoleon Bonaparte becomes Emperor.
Spain declares war on Britain.

1805 The Battle of Trafalgar. Death of Nelson.

1807 Slave trade abolished in Britain.
Napoleon Bonaparte controls all of continental Europe.

1811 Due to illness, George III is relieved of his rule and his son, the Prince of Wales becomes Regent.

Seaford Town Hall at this time

Seaford Events

George III
1760 – 1811
(cont.)

1790	Bishopstone Place, a country house of the Duke of Newcastle is advertised as 'to lett'.
	West House is advertised as a boarding school for young gentlemen, run by the Rev.G.Jenkin.
1791	James Hurdis, vicar of Bishopstone who resides at Norton House begins his exchange of letters with Cowper and himself prints his poem 'The favourite Village' at Bishopstone.
1793	Thomas Harben, Bailiff, personally takes an address from the people of Seaford to the King.
1794	Thomas Harben raises a Volunteer Corps in Seaford.
	Foundations are laid for Blatchington Barracks, on the coast near to the Battery.
	The Wiltshire Militia, under canvas at Seaford, have their tents blown away in a sudden squall during the night leaving all the men naked in the pouring rain.
1795	Prince Charles, Duke of Richmond (Lord Lieutenant of the County and descendant of Charles II) becomes Bailiff of the town but does not complete his year of office.
	Mutiny by the Oxford Militia.
1796	John Costick falls to his death while collecting gulls eggs on the cliffs.
1797	Samuel Potter is tried before T.H.Harben for felony and is sentenced to 7 years transportation.
1800	The last recorded instance of duelling in Seaford.
	The ship 'Brazen' sinks in the bay with loss of all hands.
1801	The first national census shows Seaford with a population of 847.
1804	Two carrots pulled at Seaford weigh 11lbs!
1805	Building starts on the Martello Tower.
	The future Prince Regent visits Seaford.
1806	Cuckmere Customs and Excise Station is set up.
1809	Seven ships are wrecked in Seaford Bay in a single night.

National and Other Events

During the reign of the Prince of Wales as Regent (m. Caroline of Brunswick)

1811	Luddite riots.
1812	Destruction of Napoleon's Grand Army – Retreat from Moscow. Britain at war with America.
1815	Battle of Waterloo. Steam ships on the Thames.

During the reign of George IV (m. Caroline of Brunswick)

1820	The Prince Regent is crowned King George IV following the death of his father George III. Royal Pavilion in Brighton completed (Nash).
1821	Death of Napoleon Bonaparte.
1824	Repeal of the Combination Acts which had forbidden Trades Unions.
1825	Opening of the first railway from Stockton to Darlington.
1829	Establishment of the Metropolitan Police.

During the reign of William IV (m. Adelaide of Saxe-Meiningen)

1830	Belgium breaks away from Holland.
1831	Faraday discovers electromagnetic induction.
1832	Deaths of Walter Scott and Goethe. Morse invents the electric telegraph.
1833	First British Factory Act. First government grants to English schools.
1835	Introduction of the word "Socialism".
1836	Texas independence from Mexico. Great Treck of Boers.

Seaford Events

The Regency
1811 - 1820

1811   The census shows the population to be 1001.
1812   T.H.Harben sells Corsica Hall to Mr Pinder, prospective parliamentary candidate for Seaford.
         Seaford is described as a 'Fashionable Watering Place' in the Sussex Weekly Advertiser.

George IV
1820 - 1830

1821   Census shows a population of 1047.
1823   Corsica Hall is rebuilt by the Fitzgerald Family.
1824   Another great flood inundates the town.
1825   Charles Rose Ellis is raised to the peerage with the title of Baron Seaford.

William IV
1830 - 1837

1831   Bishopstone Place is demolished as no owner could be found for it.
         Census shows population of 1098.
1832   The Reform Bill disenfranchises Seaford.
1835   Chyngton Barn is destroyed by an incendiary during agricultural unrest.
         A petition is sent to Lord Palmerston requesting a new harbour in Seaford Bay.

National and Other Events

During the reign of Victoria (m. Albert of Saxe-Coburg-Gotha)

1838 National Gallery opened.

1839 Start of the first Afghan war.

1840 The Queen marries Prince Albert. Start of postage stamps (Penny Black). Last convicts landed in Australia.

1841 Britain acquires Hong Kong.

1847 British Museum opened.

1848 Marx and Engels produce The Communist Manifesto.

1851 The Great Exhibition in the Crystal Palace in Hyde Park. First submarine telegraph cable between Dover and Calais.

1854 Crimean War.

1857 Indian Mutiny.

1859 Darwin publishes the "Origin of Species".

1861 Start of the American Civil War. Death of Prince Albert.

1865 William Booth founds the Salvation Army. Lincoln assassinated. Lister introduces antiseptic surgery in Glasgow.

1867 America purchases Alaska from Russia.

Victoria
1837 - 1901

Seaford Events

1841 Census shows population of 953.
1845 The Duke of Wellington reputed to visit Seaford. (Corroboration not found in his personal records.)
1850 Cliffs at Seaford Head are blown out to try to protect beach from erosion.
1851 Census shows population of 997.
1858 First deed of Fitzgerald Almshouses is executed.
1859 A convalescent home is established at Talland House.
1860 The Seaside Convalescent Home is established in Seaford. The first of its kind in England.
Telsemaure, a large private house is built on the seafront by Thomas Crook.
A private gas company is set up by the Crook family.
1861 Census shows population of 1094
1862 Substantial alterations are carried out on St Leonard's Church changing its proportions and mediaeval character east of the nave.
1864 The railway reaches Seaford.
The alterations to the church are completed.
1865 The first sea wall is built. (It lasts only 10 years.)
1866 Mr Bull runs the school for young gentlemen at West House.
1871 Census shows population of 1357.
1875 A really disastrous flood hits Seaford largely demolishing the sea wall.
Mr Bull removes his school from West House to the safety of Broad Street.
1877 The Congregational Church is built at the corner of Broad Street and Clinton Place.
1879 Robert Lambe obtains permission to build Claremont Road.
1880 A petition by 44 signatories is made to the Bailiff, William Webb-Turner, asking for measures to be taken to make Seaford more attractive to visitors.
Corsica Hall and its surrounding land on the market for £13,000.

National and Other Events

During the reign of Victoria (m. Albert of Saxe-Coburg-Gotha) (cont.)

1869   Formal opening of the Suez Canal.

1870   Irish Land Act. Primary education available for all children in Britain.

1872   Introduction of secret ballot in Britain.

1876   Bell invents the telephone. Death of General Custer. Queen becomes Empress of India.

1878   Cyprus leased to Britain (annexed in 1914). Second Afghan war (ended 1880). Invention of the light bulb.

1881   Pasteur demonstrates immunisation.

1884   International recognition of the Greenwich meridian.

1886   Daimler produces his first motor car.

1887   Queen Victoria's Golden Jubilee (June 21)

1888   County Councils set up in Britain.

1890   Opening of the Forth bridge. Heligoland ceded by Britain to Germany.

1895   Marconi sends a wireless message over a mile. Röntgen discovers X-rays. First work by Freud on psycho-analysis.

1899   Start of the Boer War.

1900   Proclamation of the Australian Commonwealth. Founding of the Labour Party.

Seaford Events

Victoria
1837 - 1901
(cont.)

1881	Census shows a population of 1674.
	A new sea wall is started with the first section completed in 6 months.
1884	Major Lewis T Crook is elected as Bailiff. Seaford College founded.
1885	The Last election for Bailiff is held.
1886	The Corporation of Seaford ends after an existence of 600 years.
1891	Census shows population of 1991.
	The Esplanade Hotel is built beside the old Assembly Rooms. (Demolished in 1974)
1893	The lamplighter, applying for more pay, is awarded 1s.4d (7p) per night except for the two nights before and two nights after the new moon.
	Plans are put before parliament for a pier off Seaford opposite the Esplanade Hotel; to be 600ft long.
1894	Seaford Urban District Council comes into being.
1895	The SS Seaford is lost off Beachy Head. The light ship Warner is also lost.
1898	Newhaven – Seaford Sea Defence Act to authorise construction of sea defences.
1899	The Peruvian is wrecked on the beach by the Esplanade Hotel. The International is also lost.
1900	The Aurela and The Sagatun are both lost off Seaford.

National and Other Events

During the reign of Edward VII (m. Princess Alexandra of Denmark)

1901 Opening of the Trans-Siberian Railway. Marconi sends first transatlantic wireless message.
1902 Treaty of Vereeniging ends the Boer War. Death of Cecil Rhodes.
1903 First heavier than air flight by the Wright brothers. Edward VII proclaimed Emperor of India in Delhi.
1905 Norway separates itself from Sweden. Aspirin on sale. Albert Einstein theory of relativity.
1906 Earthquake destroys San Francisco. Liberal majority in Britain. First Labour MPs. Start of Boy Scouts.
1909 Old Age Pensions in Britain. Blériot makes first cross channel flight. Ford model T mass production.

During the reign of George V (m. Princess Mary of Teck)

1910 Death of Florence Nightingale.
1912 Scott's team dies returning from the South Pole. Sinking of the Titanic.
1914 Start of "The Great War".
1916 British Summer Time introduced
1917 Revolution in Russia
1918 End of the war. Women over 30 get the vote in Britain. Founding of the Royal Air Force.
1919 First direct flight across the Atlantic. Rutherford splits the atom. Sinn Fein proclaim a separate Irish republic.
1920 First meeting of the League of Nations. Degrees first open for women at Oxford.
1921 Heavy fighting in Dublin.
1922 Mussolini's Fascist "March on Rome". Formation of the BBC. British troops leave the Irish Free State.
1924 Death of Lenin. First Labour government in Britain (falls after 11 months). Greece becomes a republic.
1926 General strike in Britain. Birth of Princess Elizabeth.
1928 Alexander Fleming discovers Penicillin. Women get the same voting rights as men. Introduction of £1 and 10s notes.
1929 Wall Street Crash.
1933 Hitler becomes German Chancelor
1934 Hitler becomes dictator. Introduction of driving tests. Chinese army "Long March".
1935 War between Italy and Abyssinia. Baldwin becomes Prime Minister. Invention of radar.

Seaford Events

Edward VII
1901 - 1910

1901 Census shows population of 2615.
Sarah Crook, wife of the first owner of Telsemaure dies aged 93; she is much mourned and remembered for her charitable works in the town.
1905 Newlands School set up on its present site.
1906 Seaford Gasworks taken over as a public company.
1907 Sutton Mill pulled down after 138 years.
1909 Major Crook leaves Seaford and is given a farewell dinner and Address at the Wellington Hotel.

George V
1910 - 1936

1911 Census shows population of 3683.
1912 The Empire Cinema is built in Sutton Road.
1914 North and South army camps are built to house troops during the war, including many Canadians and West Indians.
A seaplane base is built at Tide Mills.
1921 Census shows population of 5249.
1928 Seaford Urban District Council purchases Seaford Head and Golf Links for £16,527.
1931 Census shows population of about 7000.
1933 The Stud Farm Aerodrome is run by London and Provincial Aviation Ltd.
1935 Place House, on junction of Place Lane and Broad Street is demolished after 302 years.

National and Other Events

During the reign of Edward VIII (Never crowned)

1936 Hitler opens a factory for making the people's car (Volkswagen).
Civil war in Spain. BBC first talking television transmission. Crystal Palace burns down.
Edward VIII abdicates taking the title of Duke of Windsor. His brother, Bertie succeeds him as George VI.

During the reign of George VI (m. Lady Elizabeth Bowes-Lyon – Later the Queen Mother)

1937 First frozen food in Britain. Introduction of the 999 emergency number.
1938 Germany annexes Austria. Kristallnacht.
1939 Spanish Civil War ends. Germany invades Poland leading to outbreak of World War II.
1940 Start of rationing in Britain. Germany invades Denmark, Norway, Netherlands, Belgium and France. Battle of Britain and start of the Blitz.
1941 Germany invades Bulgaria and Russia but Russia pushes the German army back during the winter. Japan attacks Pearl Harbour bring the USA into the war.
1943 Germany starts to lose in Russia and North Africa. Mussolini flees as allies land in Italy.
1944 Allied forces land in Normandy. Paris is liberated.
1945 Germany surrenders. USA drops atom bombs on Hiroshima and Nagasaki. End of World War II. Founding of the United Nations.
1946 League of Nations formally wound up and succeeded by the UNO. Bread rationed in Britain.
1947 Princess Elizabeth married Phillip.
1948 Partition of Palestine to form Israel. Assassination of Mahatma Gandhi. Invention of the transistor.
1949 Formation of NATO.
1950 Start of the Korean War - ends 1953. Start of "The Archers".
1951 The Festival of Britain. Burgess & Maclean defect.

Seaford Events

Edward VIII
1936 - 1936

1936   Foundation is laid for the Ritz Cinema at junction of Dane Road and Pelham Road. Telsemaure is demolished after 96 years. Russian cargo ship *"Ussuri"* beached at Seaford.

George VI
1936 - 1952

1938   Bishopstone Station is opened.
1939   Empire Cinema burned down.
1940   Seaford College leaves Seaford.
1942   Tide Mills is used for close combat training and is reduced to rubble. Bombs are dropped on Pelham Place in one of the worst air raids on the Town.
1945   Disastrous 4 day storm damage to sea wall. Repairs and more damage to 1947.
1946   Visit by Mrs Winston Churchill. Broadcast of "In Town Tonight"
1948   Sea defences breached. Sea wall refaced. Further repairs over the next year.
1950   £10,000 sea defence scheme started. Corsica Hall as Home Economics College.
1951   Celebration of the Festival of Britain included talent competition concert at Queen's Hall, table-tennis tournament at Clinton Hall and an exhibition of paintings at Seaford Training College (Corsica Hall). "Down Your Way" from Seaford. Champion Radio factory in Seaford burnt down.

National and Other Events

During the reign of Elizabeth II (m. Philip Mountbatten formerly Prince Philip of Greece)

1952   Last London tram. Heavy smog in London. Death of Eva Peron. Mau Mau in Kenya.

1953   Death of Stalin. Launch of the *Britannia*. First ascent of Mount Everest. End of the Korean War. Beria executed. Death of Queen Mary. Coronation of Queen Elizabeth II. Piltdown man hoax exposed.

1954   End of food rationing in Britain. Roger Bannister 4 minute mile. The European Convention on Human Rights.

1955   Blue jeans craze in Britain. Civil war in Vietnam. Riots in Algeria and Morocco. Start of ITV.

1956   The Suez crisis. Premium Bonds introduced. Polish & Hungarian anti-Soviet revolts Pakistan in the Commonwealth. Israel invasion of Egypt taking Sinai. Alabama race riots. Flood of Hungarian refugees in Britain.

1957   Treaty of Rome starts the European Common Market. Russia launches the first artificial satellite *'Sputnik 1'*. State of emergency against IRA in Irish Republic. Asian Flu. Myxamatosis. Little Rock.

1958   CND founded. First heart pacemaker implant.. First US satellite. Prince Charles becomes Prince of Wales (see 1969). First hovercraft. Opening of Gatwick airport. Notting Hill race riots. Thalidomide.

1959   Fidel Castro overthrows Batista in Cuba. Dalai Lama flees Llasa. St Lawrence Seaway opened. First Mini. First moon landing by Soviet *Lunik II*. Britain's first motorway M1 opened.

1960   "New Franc" in France. *"Lady Chatterley's Lover"* trial. End of National Service in Britain. End of the farthing.

1961   First Polaris submarines at Holy Loch. First betting shops in Britain. Tristan da Cunha volcano – whole population shipped to Britain. First USA manned space flight. Soviets seal off East Berlin.

1962   First live TV between USA and Europe. Cuban missile crisis.

1963   Beeching report. Great train robbery. Dartford tunnel opened. Assassination of President Kennedy.

1964   Death of Nehru. First GLC elections. Start of BBC-2. Nelson Mandela jailed for life. New Forth Bridge.

1965   Death of Winston Churchill. Start of Vietnam War North Sea oil. UDI in Rhodesia. Start of 70 mph speed limits.

1966   England won World Cup. Aberfan disaster. New Severn road bridge.

1967   Israel starts 6 day war. Start of colour TV in Britain on BBC-2. First human heart transplant. Launch of QE2. End of steam engines on BR Southern Region. Sweden's traffic changed to drive on the right.

1968   Assassination of Martin Luther King. Start of 1st / 2nd class post in Britain. Start of more troubles in N.Ireland.

1969   Maiden flights of Concord (French & British). Opening of the Victoria Line. Voting age 18. First men on the Moon. Investiture of Prince of Wales. End of halfpennies, introduction of 50p (10 shilling) piece.

**Elizabeth II
1952 -**

Seaford Events

1952	Resiting of the War Memorial from Dane Road to present site.
1953	Grant of arms to SUDC. Fitting of the Coronation Gate at Crouch Gardens.
1954	Sea wall damaged.
1955	Pilgrim's School opened by HRH Princess Margaret
1956	Sea wall damaged.
1957	Another sea defence scheme.
1959	Seaford Residents' Association founded.
1960	Special meeting between UDC, Newhaven & Seaford Sea Defence Commission and Seaford Residents Association to calm residents' concern about the sea wall and sea defences.
1962	The old Buckle Inn is demolished and New Buckle built to replace it further from the shore. Buckle bypass developed.
1964	Talland House is demolished after 250 years. Seaford Urban District Offices move to The Downs. Rail goods service ends.
1965	The Old Tree Inn, on corner of High Street and Broad Street is demolished after 387 years.
1966	New Constitutional Club opened by William Whitelaw.
1967	New Golf Clubhouse opened in Southdown Road.
1969	New Police Station opens in Church Street. Major fire at Golden Galleon.

The Coronation Gate at Crouch Gardens
The arch came from the old Town Hall (see page 44)

National and Other Events

During the reign of Elizabeth II (m. Philip Mountbatten formerly Prince Philip of Greece) (cont.)

1970 New English Bible. *Apollo 13* rescue. *SS Great Britain* moved from Falklands to Bristol. Death of Gen. De Gaulle.
1971 Idi Amin takes power in Uganda. Collapse of Rolls Royce. Women get voting rights in Switzerland. European currency crisis. Start of decimal currency in Britain. Short Indo-Pakistan war.
1972 Londonderry "Bloody Sunday". Miners strike and many other disputes cause power cuts and chaos in Britain. Ceylon became Sri Lanka. Death of the Duke of Windsor. Watergate.
1973 Britain joins EEC. Introduction of VAT. IRA bombs in London. Cod War. Oil crisis.
1974 Turkish invasion of Cyprus. Anti-Terrorism Bill after May IRA bombings in Britain.
1975 End of Vietnam war. Juan Carlos becomes king of Spain. Sex Discrimination and Equal Pay Acts.
1976 End of Cod War. Opening of the National Theatre.
1977 Extension of fishing rights to 200 miles. Silver Jubilee celebrations. Uganda massacres. 60 mph limit off motorways.
1978 *Ekofisk Bravo* oil platform disaster. Israel attack Lebanon. Start of May Day holiday. First "Test Tube" baby.
1979 Shah left Iran. Margaret Thatcher became first woman PM. Queen Mother installed as Warden of the Cinque Ports.
1980 Robert Mugabe leader in Rhodesia (Zimbabwe). Queen Beatrix invested in the Netherlands. Iranian Embassy hostages Opening of St Gotthard road tunnel. Iran/Iraq war.
1981 First Sunday Football League. Launch of Social Democratic Party. First London marathon. Riots in many cities. Marriage of Prince Charles to Diana Spencer.
1982 Barbican Centre opened. Argentina invaded Falkland Islands. Raising of the *"Mary Rose"*. Start of Channel-4 TV. Greenham Common protest started.
1983 Seat belts compulsory. Shergar. First wheel clamps. US invaded Grenada. Launch of European *Spacelab*.
1984 Many coal mines closed. Libyan Embassy siege. Gulf war. York Minster fire. IRA bomb Grand Hotel in Brighton.
1985 Heysel football stadium disaster led to ban on English teams and fans. *Rainbow Warrior* sinking.
1986 Shuttle *"Challenger"* disaster. Chernobyl disaster. Launch of *"The Independent"*. M25 completed.
1987 Zeebrugge ferry capsized. Princess Anne titled Princess Royal. Hurricane. Black Monday stock crash.
1988 Russia withdraws from Afghanistan. *PiperAlpha* oil rig disaster. All day opening for pubs. Lockerbie.
1989 Hillsborough disaster. Tiananmen Square. Death of Khomeni. Collapse of Communist governments in Europe. End of Berlin Wall. US invaded Panama. End of Cold War.

Seaford Events

Elizabeth II
1952 -
(cont.)

1970	Seaford Museum of Local History is founded. The collection was initially in a caravan. Seaford Lifeguards founded.
1971	Census shows a population of 16,226. BBC "Any Questions" from Seaford.
1972	The Baptist Church in Broad Street is demolished. *"Walter Richter"* shipwrecked at Tidemills.
1974	The end of Seaford Urban District Council. Seaford becomes part of Lewes District.
1975	Railway reduced to single track from Newhaven.
1976	Archeological dig in Church Street.
1977	Peter White appointed Town Crier. Ladycross School closed.
1978	Superstructure (a flat) removed from the Martello Tower.
1979	Seaford Museum moves into the Martello tower.
1980	First Town Council referendum. Princess Margaret visits Pilgrims School.
1981	The population of Seaford is 17,785. Rebuilding/extensions to Methodist Church in Steyne Road.
1982	St Peter's School closed.
1983	*"Seahaven News"* weekly paper started. Barn Theatre created.
1984	Twinning with Bönningstedt. Building of Catholic Church Hall.
1985	Start of Neighbourhood Watch in Seaford.
1986	Sainsburys (Broad St.) closes. Safeway opens on Ritz Cinema Site.
1987	The recharging of Seaford beach takes place. Hurricane destroys Baptist Church roof and causes much local damage.
1988	Old Golf Clubhouse in Chyngton Road demolished and redeveloped.
1989	Major fire in the old Town Hall in South Street.

National and Other Events

During the reign of Elizabeth II (m. Philip Mountbatten formerly Prince Philip of Greece) (cont.)

1990 Collapse of Soviet Union. Nelson Mandela released from 25 years jail. IRA bombings. German re-unification, Iraq invaded Kuwait. End of Cambodian civil war. Britain alone against Monetary Union. Recession in Britain.

1991 Operation Desert Storm. End of Poll Tax. End of apartheid in S. Africa. Ethnic fighting in Serbia, Croatia, Sri Lanka, E.Timor, Bosnia-Herzegovina.

1992 N. & S. Korea end 40 year confrontation. Betty Boothroyd first woman Speaker of Commons. UN forces in Somalia. Collapse of £ Britain withdraws from ERM. Angolan war. Windsor fire. Prince & Princess of Wales separate.

1993 Riots in Kinshasa. Ethnic cleansing continued in Croatia & Bosnia. Buckingham Palace opened to the public. Establishment of the European Union.

1994 Massacres in Rwanda. Nelson Mandela president in S.Africa. Channel tunnel opened. "Cash for Questions" scandal. Comet Shoemaker-Levy. National Lottery. Arrest of "The Jackal". Russia invaded Chechnya. EU workers' rights.

1995 Austria, Finland & Sweden join EU. Kobe earthquake. Animal Rights protests. Collapse of Barings Bank. Ethnic clashes in Burundi. Riots in Luton. Drought affects a third of Britain. Pre-packed food sold by metric weight.

1996 End of IRA ceasefire. Dunblane massacre. British beef export bans (BSE). Russian ceasefire in Chechenya.

1997 Death of Princess Diana. Hong Kong handed back to China.

1998 Serbs battle ethnic Albanians in Kosovo. Good Friday Accord. Augusto Pinochet arrested in London. India atomic tests. White House sex scandal. Clinton orders air strikes on Iraq.

1999 Death of King Hussein of Jordan. First nonstop balloon flight around world. "Melissa" computer virus. Self rule in N. Ireland.

2000 Hijackers seize Afghan plane & release hostages in Stansted. Concorde crash near Paris. BSE scares in Europe.

2001 Sept. 11 Islamic attacks in USA lead to Afghan war.

2002 The Euro becomes the currency for most of Europe. Deaths of H.R.H. Princess Margaret and H.M. Queen Elizabeth the Queen Mother in the first part of this Golden Jubilee Year of H.M. the Queen.

Seaford Events

Elizabeth II
1952 -
(cont.)

1990	Celebration of 900 years of St Leonard's Church.
1991	Census shows a population of 20,933.
1992	Seaford County Primary School moves to Wilkinson Way.
1993	Improvements to High Street with paving, street lamps, etc.
1994	Opening of the Crypt Gallery.
1995	Fifth and final vote for Town Council. Seaford Film Society founded.
1997	Len Fisher appointed Town Manager.
1998	First "Clean Beach" award.
	Dutch sailing ship *"Eendracht"* runs aground in a storm at Tidemills.
1999	Seaford elects its first Town Council and Mayor is appointed.
	CCTV system installed in the town centre.
2000	Purchase of Hurdis House in Broad Street for the Town Council.
2001	Flood lighting on St Leonard's Church.
2002	Town Council granted use of the Seaford Coat of Arms (see page 1)
	Demolition of first Baptist Chapel in South Street and houses built.

Seaford Museum of Local History

Seaford Museum is housed in Martello Tower number 74 on the eastern seafront in Seaford, East Sussex, England. The Museum is run entirely by volunteer staff and there are fascinating collections of household and office equipment and tableaux depicting typical Victorian shops and home life with original artefacts in realistic surroundings. The Martello Tower itself is very interesting, being the last of a series of towers built as defence against Napoleon in 1810. Half of the dry moat around the tower was covered in 1935 to form a continuation of the promenade along the seafront. This formed a large covered space in half of the moat, which is now the main display area of the Museum.

Registered Museum Number 1497   Registered Charity Number 272864

SEAFORD MUSEUM and HERITAGE SOCIETY
Martello Tower – The Esplanade – Seaford – East Sussex
Postal address: c/o Tourist Information Centre,
25 Clinton Place, Seaford, East Sussex BN25 1NP
Tel: 01323-898222   E-mail: museumseaford@tinyonline.co.uk   Web-site: www.seafordmuseum.org

Notes:

Notes: